YOU MIGHT BE FROM NOVA SCOTIA IF...

Michael de Adder

MacIntyre Purcell Publishing Inc.
194 Hospital Rd.
Lunenburg, Nova Scotia
B0J 2C0
(902) 640-2337

www.macintyrepurcell.com
info@macintyrepurcell.com

Printed and bound by Marquis.

Library and Archives Canada Cataloguing in Publication

De Adder, Michael, 1967- [Cartoons. Selections]
You might be from Nova Scotia if... / Michael de Adder.

MacIntyre Purcell Publishing Inc. would like to acknowledge the financial support of the Government of Canada through Department of Canadian Heritage (Canada Book Fund) and the Nova Scotia Department of Tourism, Culture and Heritage.

FOR BRIDGET

FOREWORD

Be afraid . . . no, be really afraid of these guys . . . these cartoonists; they skulk about on editorial sections and pin poor public figures to pages of smudgy newsprint.

Be honest now, though; you flip through the paper . . . and landing at the op-ed page, you might read the header on the editorial, "Canada Must Cling to Niceness", but you don't read it; you see the 5,000 word "think piece" on Maritime Union, but jeeze who's wading through that?

There are three columnists willing to tell you what you should think about matters in the news, but you'd really rather do your own thinking. BUT de Adder's got a cartoon of Harper gulping oil sand petro products . . . you see it, you get it, and depending on your politics and/or sense of humor love it or hate it.

There is something about the fusion of an image and a message in a cartoon that gives it such impact. Long after a politician leaves the stage . . . long after an event has passed into history you can often conjure up the memory of a drawing in a newspaper which captured the person or the event in a way that mere words don't or can't.

As I sit at my desk, off to the left on the wall is a cartoon of the *Information Morning* crew of the early eighties (by another talented Nova Scotian). I see it every day and realize that the drawing (with me hooked up to a coffee intravenous drip) is a perfect snapshot of an era in our lives.

Michael has over a long period of time captured important, happy and poignant moments in the life of the province. Keep it up de Adder . . . and leave me out of it.

— Don Connolly, host of Information Morning

INTRODUCTION

I grew up travelling to both New Glasgow and the Annapolis Valley (my mother is from Westville and my father is from Kentville). I'm proud to say they are my stomping grounds. With and through aunts, uncles, cousins and friends I feel as if I've travelled to every corner of Nova Scotia.

The family members who listened and offered suggestions included Lori MacDonald, Erin Dwyer, Mark MacDonald, Sherri Joyce Karn and friend of the family, Leslie MacDonald. I'd like to thank Chris Joyce, Kathy Barrie and Natalie Dwyer-Edinger for lending an ear to the discussion. And special thanks go to Paul De Adder and David De Adder for performing their roles as brothers and openly mocking me at every turn.

Of the friends I contacted I'd like to thank Shaune MacKinlay who probably could have written her own book. David Rodenhiser made a lot of very funny suggestions, but unfortunately for Dave it's not that kind of book. He does, in the end, get credit for what I think is the funniest cartoon which appears on the back cover. The CHRONICLE HERALD'S Stephen Cooke was a lot of help; as were Michelle Thornhill and Jerry West.

I'd also like to thank Greg Little, Julian Marchant, Joanne Marchant, Meredith MacKinlay, John MacIntyre, Amy Jones and Lloyd Nauss.

For the Cape Breton cartoons I'd like to thank my Caper friends from my Mount Allison days, Irene MacKinnon, MaryJane MacDonald, and Laurie MacInnis-Dunn.

And last but not least, I'd like to thank my wife Gail for reading and offering suggestions and for covering for me on the weekends when I had to work on this book. I'd also like to thank my daughters Meaghan and Bridget for their understanding. Yes, girls, the book is done!

— *Michael de Adder, Nova Scotia*

YOU MIGHT BE FROM NOVA SCOTIA IF...

KITCHEN →

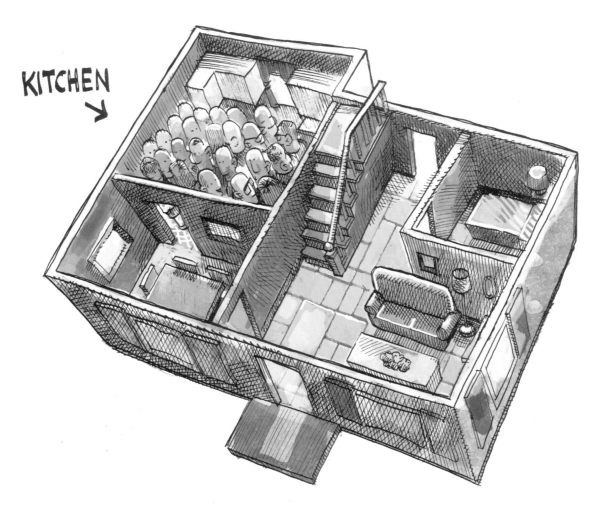

YOU ONLY USE ONE ROOM WHEN HAVING A PARTY

WHEN UNDER A HURRICANE WARNING YOU HAVE
BEER ON YOUR LIST OF ESSENTIAL SUPPLIES.

WHEN TAKING THE LORD'S NAME IN VAIN,
YOU INCLUDE HIS PARENTS.

YOU CALL THE "NEW BRIDGE" THE ONE BUILT IN 1970.

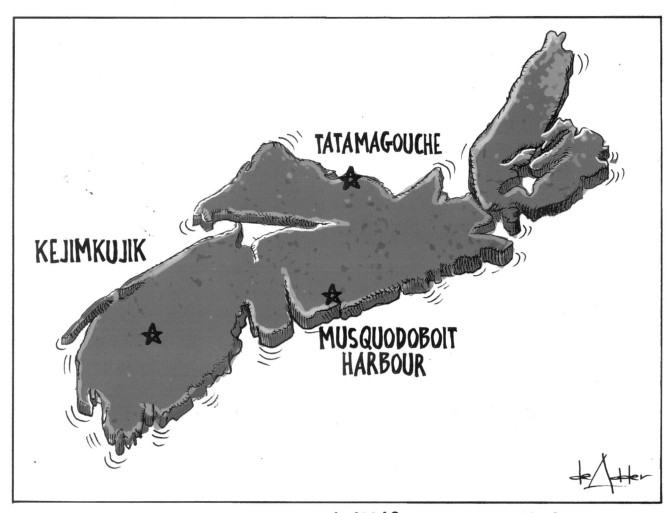

YOU CAN PRONOUNCE KEJIMKUJIK, TATAMAGOUCHE AND MUSQUODOBOIT.

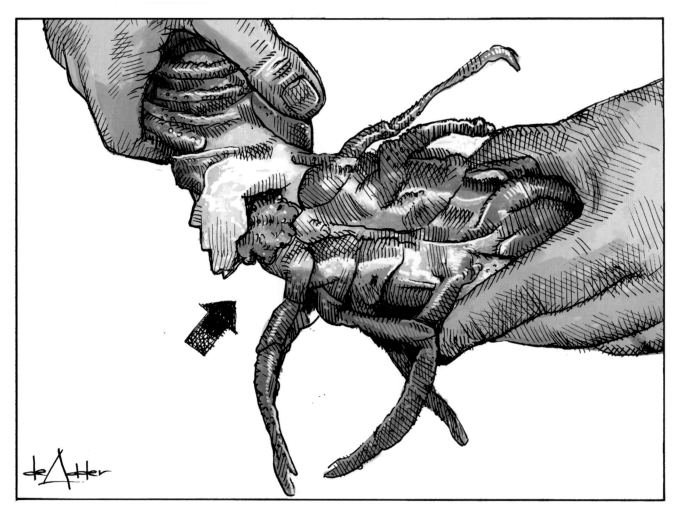

YOU EAT THE GREEN GUNK IN THE LOBSTER.

YOUR OLD RECORD COLLECTION IS HEAVY ON THE APRIL WINE.

YOU LOOK LIKE THIS WHEN SOMEBODY FROM ONTARIO GIVES THEIR OPINION ON THE ECONOMIC SITUATION IN ATLANTIC CANADA.

YOU GIVE DIRECTIONS USING PIZZA CORNER AS A REFERENCE.

YOU KNOW "SOCIABLES" AREN'T BUTTERY CRACKERS.

THAT'S SOME GOOD.

YOU USE "SOME" AS A MODIFYING ADJECTIVE.

YOU CALL THIS
"HAVING A GLOW".

YOU CALL THIS
"BEING OUT OF 'ER".

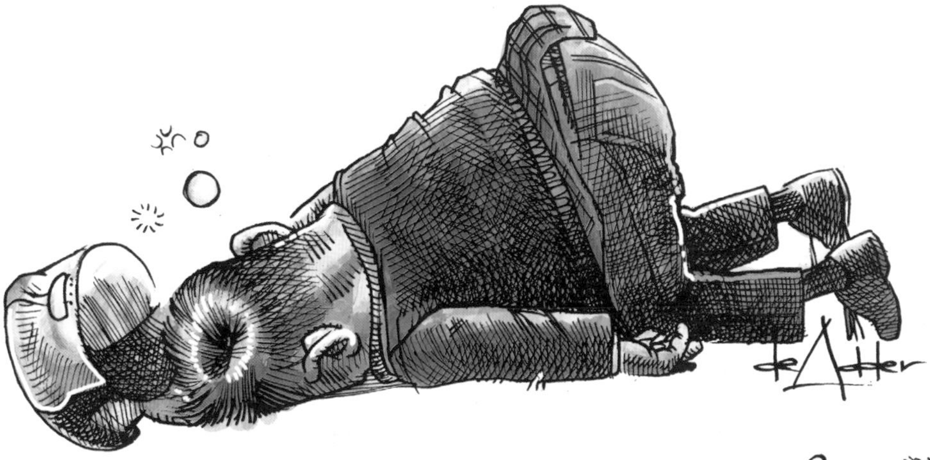

YOU CALL THIS BEING
"RIGHT OUT OF 'ER".

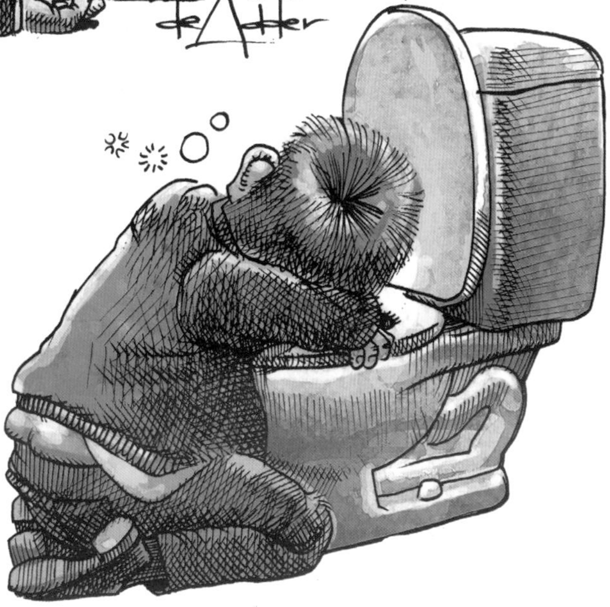

YOU CALL THIS BEING
"RIGHT SOME OUT OF 'ER".

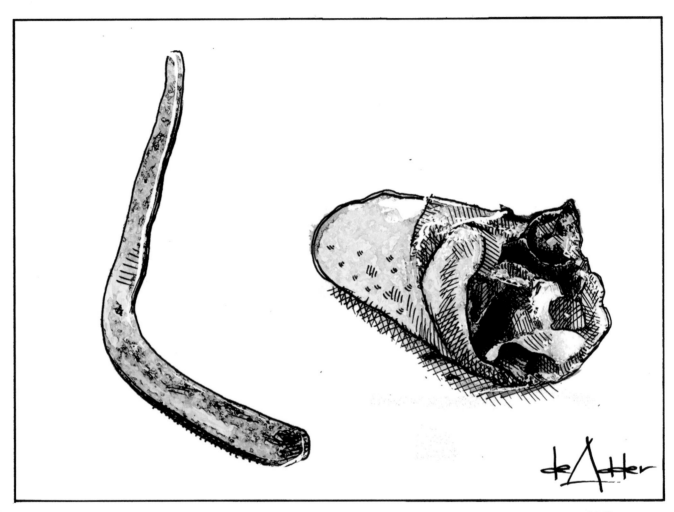

YOU KNOW THE BIRTHPLACE OF HOCKEY AND THE DONAIR.

FOR YOU THE CAT DIDN'T ALWAYS COME BACK.

YOU CONSIDER THESE TO BE THE FOUR SEASONS.

YOU CONSIDER THE SUN TO BE A RARE CELESTIAL OCCURANCE

YOU THINK AMBER MEANS GIVE'R.

YOU CAN STOP TRAFFIC SIMPLY BY STEPPING OFF THE CURB.

YOU LIKE THIS A LOT.

YOU CONSIDER THIS TO BE AN IMPORT.

YOU ONCE KNEW
SOMEBODY WHO
DRANK THESE.

YOU LOOK FOR THESE
TO MARK PEOPLE
FROM ONTARIO.

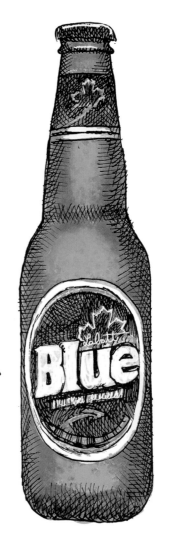

EVERYTIME FRIENDS COME FROM AWAY YOU GO TO PEGGY'S COVE.

ONTARIO

NOVA SCOTIA

YOU CAN WATCH AN AIRSHOW EVERY DAY.

YOU CHECK FOR HONEY BEES WHEN CROSSING THE BORDER.

YOU SING THE ANSWER WHENEVER ANYBODY ASKS
FOR THE NUMBER OF A CAB IN HALIFAX.

ON VACATION, YOU MEET SOMEBODY WHO KNOWS ONE OTHER PERSON FROM NOVA SCOTIA, AND YOU KNOW THAT PERSON TOO.

YOU COMPLAIN ABOUT THE PRICE OF GAS, BUT YOU WILL PAY OVER $15.00 TRYING TO WIN A FREE DONUT.

YOU'VE GONE FISHING AND THE ONLY THING YOU CAUGHT WAS A FEW ZS.

SEEING THE CANSO CAUSEWAY MEANS YOU'RE ALMOST HOME.

YOU HAVE EXPLAINED WHAT DONAIRS ARE TO PEOPLE THAT ARE NOT FROM HERE.

YOU CELEBRATE SPRING BY SHOVELING THE DRIVEWAY.

MEAT COVE, COW BAY AND ECUM SECUM SOUND LIKE ORDINARY PLACE NAMES.

YOU KNOW THAT THE DIFFERENCE BETWEEN A VIOLIN AND A FIDDLE IS THE PERSON USING IT.

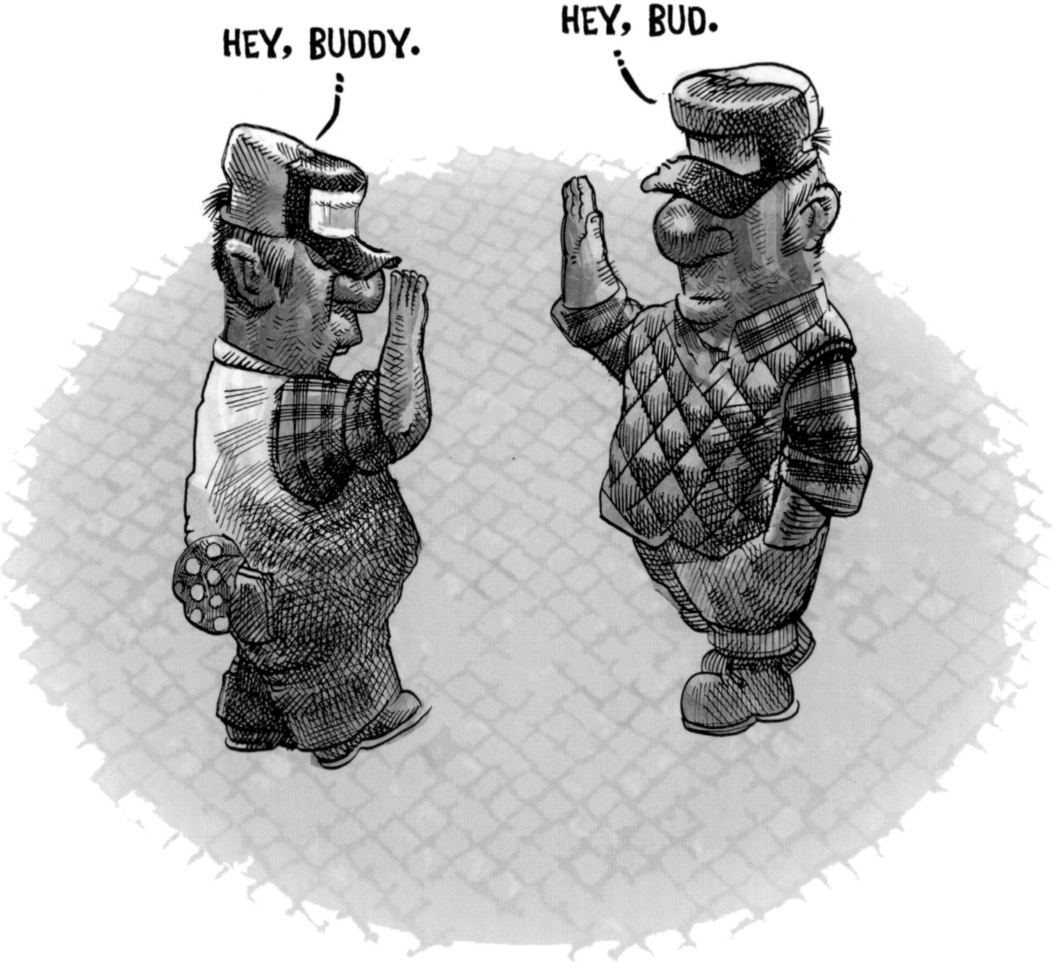
HEY, BUDDY.
HEY, BUD.

YOU CALL EVERYBODY BUDDY.

YOU USE A MASTODON AS A MILEPOST.

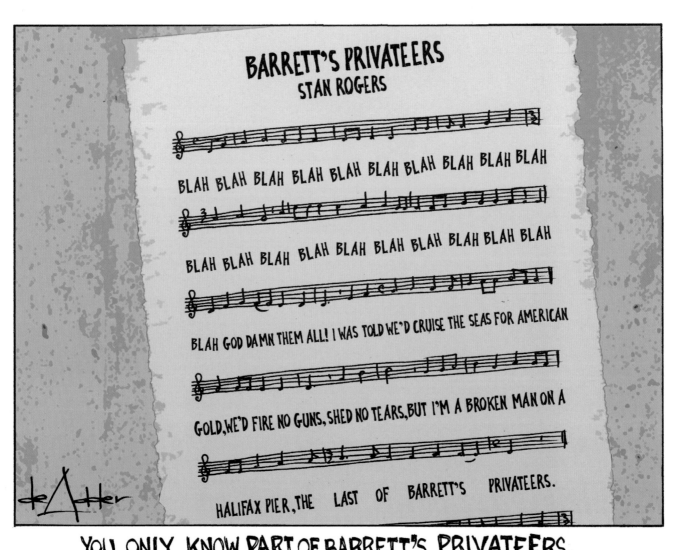

YOU ONLY KNOW PART OF BARRETT'S PRIVATEERS.

YOU KNOW THE PEI TOURISM NUMBER, BUT YOU DON'T KNOW THE ONE FOR NOVA SCOTIA.

YOU REMEMBER DON MESSER'S JUBILEE

YOU REMEMBER WHEN THE ONLY THING ON TELEVISION WAS STACEY'S COUNTRY JAMBOREE.

YOU FREAK OUT IF NOVA SCOTIA IS MENTIONED
IN AN AMERICAN MOVIE.

YOU AND YOUR NEIGHBOURS HAVE THE SAME LAST NAME.

WHEN WALKING ALONG THE HALIFAX WATERFRONT,
YOU FEEL LIKE YOU'RE BEING WATCHED.

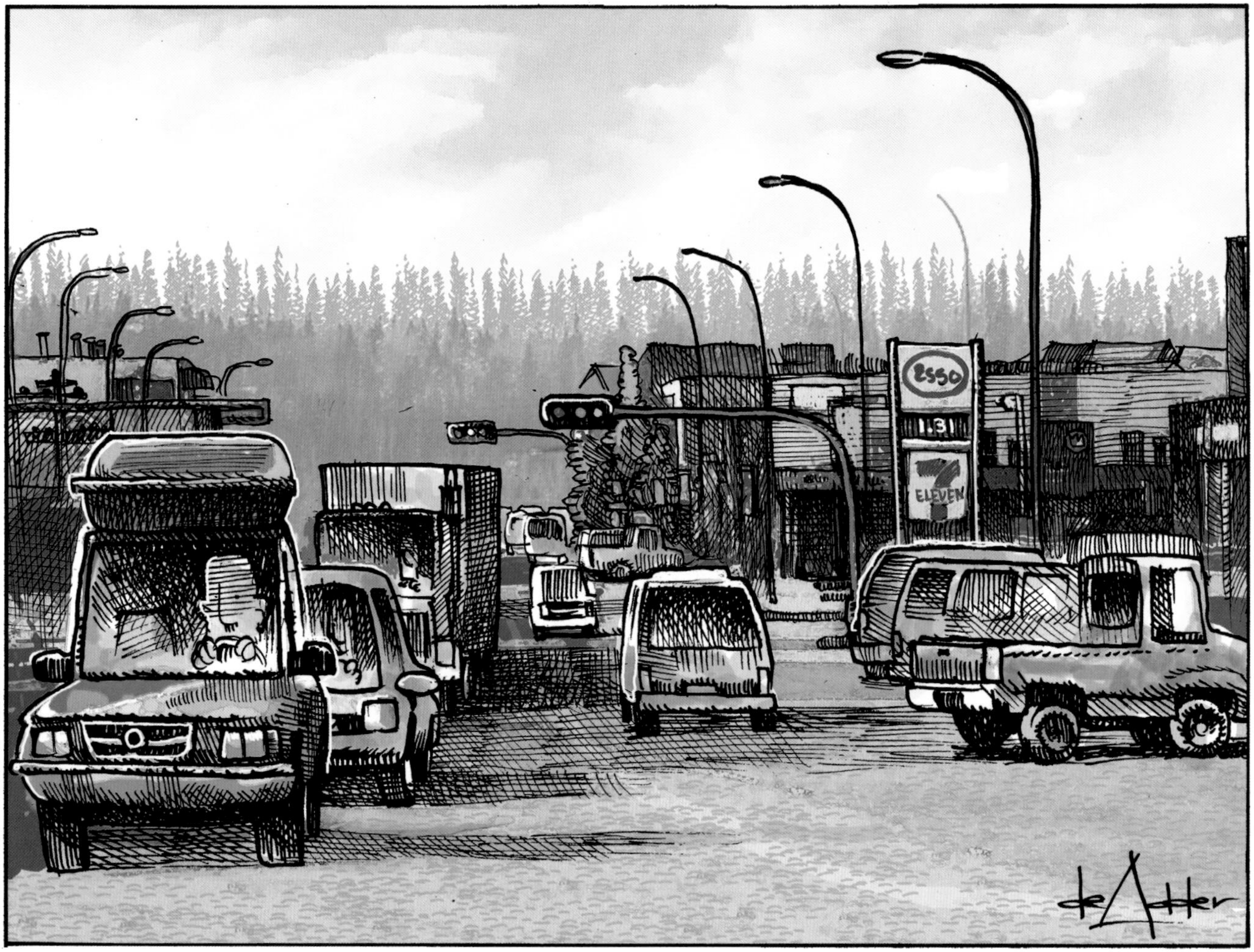
Esso
1.31
7
ELEVEN
deAdder

YOU LIVE IN FORT MAC.

YOU DON'T JUST KNOW PEOPLE LIKE THE TRAILER PARK BOYS,
YOU KNOW THE TRAILER PARK BOYS.

YOU KNOW YOUR CELEBRITIES BY THEIR FIRST NAME.

YOU HAVE SHOVELLED SNOW IN THE RAIN.

YOU HAVE RAKED LEAVES IN THE SNOW.

YOU THINK WEARING A KILT MAKES YOU LOOK LIKE WILLIAM WALLACE, BUT YOU REALLY LOOK LIKE A MAN IN A SKIRT.

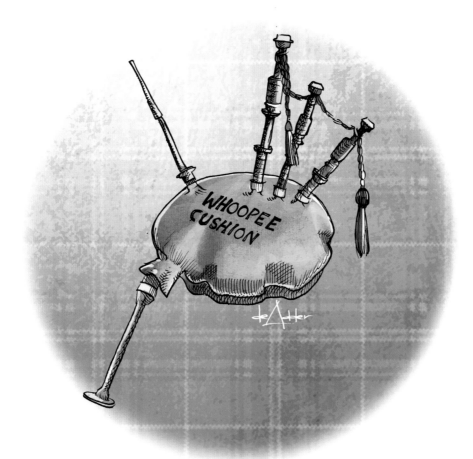

YOU LOVE THE BAGPIPES BUT CAN'T
ALWAYS TELL WHEN THEY ARE IN TUNE.

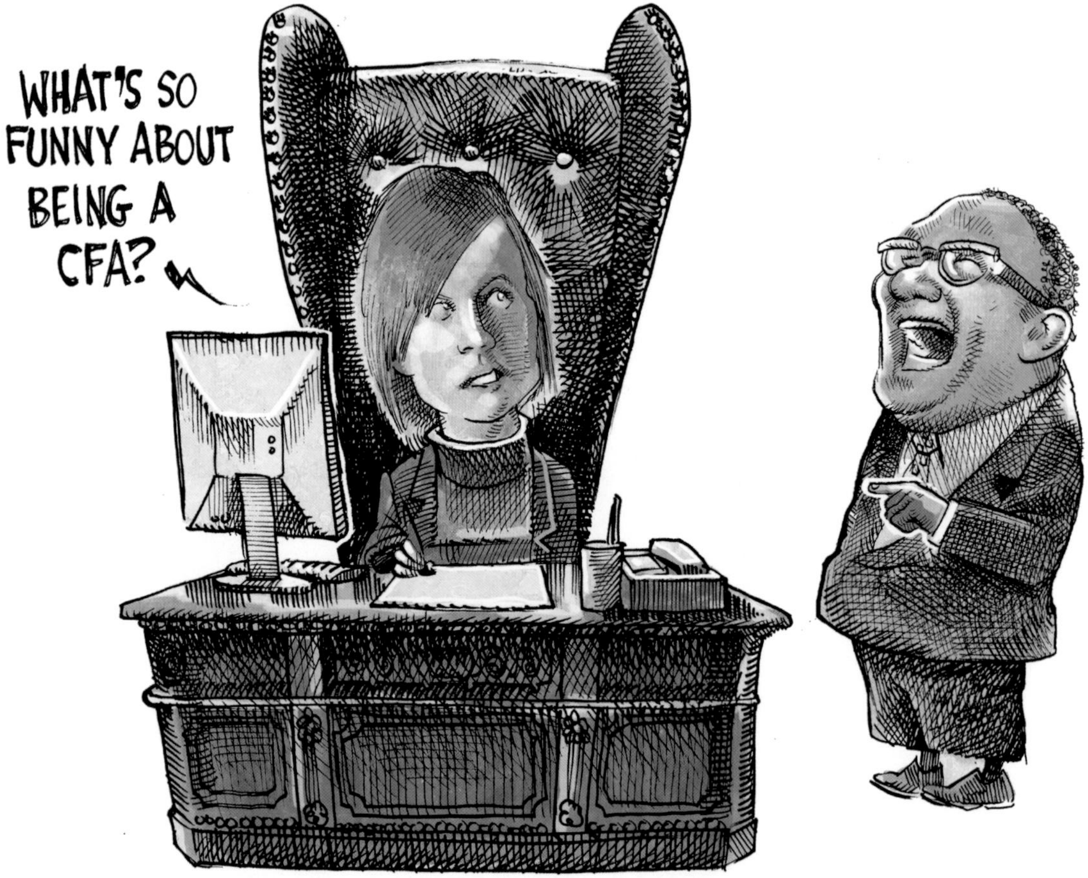
WHAT'S SO FUNNY ABOUT BEING A CFA?

YOU KNOW CFA DOESN'T STAND FOR CHARTERED FINANCIAL ANALYST.

YOU DON'T FLINCH WHEN THE NOON-DAY GUN GOES OFF IN HALIFAX.

STEP ONE OF YOUR RECIPE FOR HODGE PODGE
IS PLANTING THE VEGETABLES.

YOU GREW UP EATING BLUEBERRY GRUNT.

FRESH FRIED CLAMS

FRIED CLAM STRIPS

YOU'D TRAVEL AN HOUR OUTSIDE OF TOWN FOR GOOD FRIED CLAMS,
BUT YOU WOULDN'T CROSS THE STREET FOR CLAM STRIPS.

YOU LOOK FORWARD TO THE PLATES OF SQUARES
AFTER A WEDDING, FUNERAL, OR FAMILY REUNION.

YOU THOUGHT "BOILED DINNER" WAS DISGUSTING AS A KID, BUT FIND YOURSELF CRAVING IT AS AN ADULT.

YOU ALREADY SPILLED DONAIR SAUCE ON THIS BOOK.

YOU FEEL SORRY FOR ALL THOSE PROVINCES
THAT DON'T COME WITH AN OCEAN VIEW.

YOU TOOK A ROMANTIC CRUISE ON THE DARTMOUTH FERRY.

AS A KID, YOU SPENT HOURS ON A HALLOWEEN COSTUME
ONLY TO HAVE YOUR MOTHER MAKE YOU WEAR A COAT OVER IT.

AS AN ADULT YOU SPENT WEEKS ON A HALLOWEEN COSTUME.

YOU THINK NOVA SCOTIA'S MOST COMMON ORCHID, THE LADY SLIPPER, DOESN'T LOOK LIKE SOMETHING A LADY WOULD WEAR.

YOU LIVE IN THE ONE PROVINCE THAT HAS ABSOLUTELY
NO PROBLEM NAMING THE SHIP ON THE TEN CENT PIECE.

YOU KNOW THAT NOVA SCOTIA'S MAIN AIRPORT
ISN'T NAMED AFTER THE UNDERWEAR.

SUMMER

YOU START TO DREAD WINTER'S RETURN IN JUNE.

YOU KNOW NOVA SCOTIA'S MOST FAMOUS PAINTING IS A HOUSE.

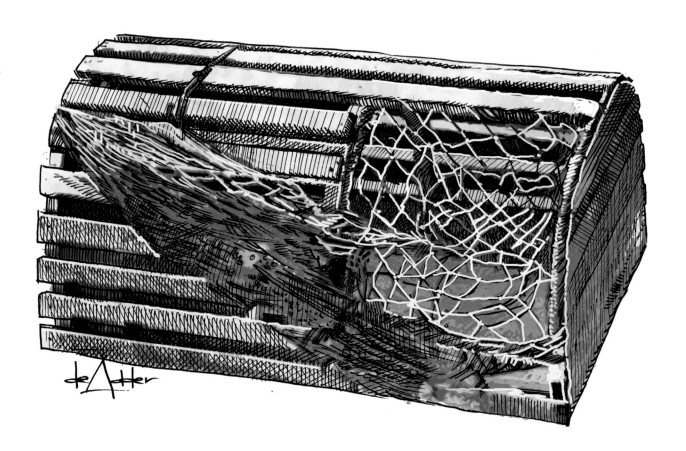

YOU CONSIDER THIS A LAWN ORNAMENT.

YOU CALL A LATE SPRING SNOW A POOR MAN'S FERTILIZER.

YOU REMAIN IN DENIAL ON THOSE COLD SUMMER DAYS.

YOU ONCE SAW ATLANTIC GRAND PRIX WRESTLING
LIVE ON A SATURDAY NIGHT IN BERWICK.

YOU'VE BEEN ON A PUB CRAWL IN A ONE PUB TOWN.

YOU NOT ONLY FARM CATTLE, YOU FARM CHRISTMAS TREES.

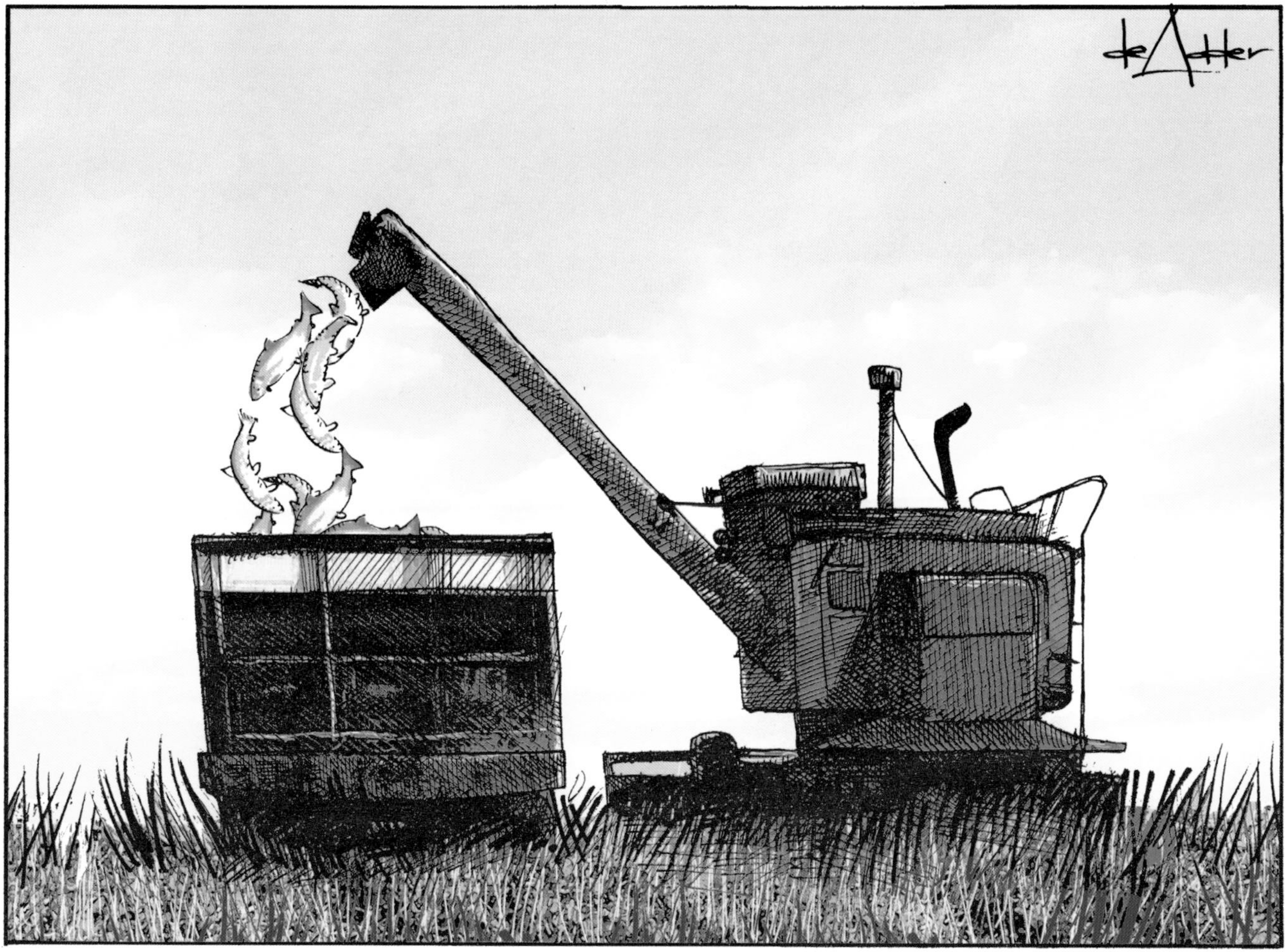
deAdder

YOU ALSO FARM SALMON.

YOU DON'T FIND IT ODD TO BUY SCALLOPS FROM THE BACK OF SOME GUYS TRUCK.

YOU DON'T TRUST YOUR GPS BUT STILL TRUST
THAT 1972 MAP YOU KEEP JUST IN CASE.

YOU STICK OUT LIKE A SORE THUMB IN NEW YORK CITY.

YOU HAVE A SNOW BLOWER AND YOU BLOW THE ENTIRE NEIGHBOURHOOD.

YOU KNOW THERE ARE TWO TYPES OF MOOSE HUNTER.
THOSE WHO GOT THEIR MOOSE LICENCE AND THOSE
WHO THINK THE MOOSE DRAW IS RIGGED.

YOU FIND NOTHING WRONG WITH EATING DULCE.

YOU KNOW WHY THERE'S A WASHING MACHINE IN THE SPORTS HALL OF FAME.

FOR YOU VIMY, ORTONA, AND NORMANDY AREN'T JUST PLACES ON A MAP.

YOU KNOW SOMEBODY WHO ALWAYS GOES 30 FOR 60.

YOU'VE SEEN A LIGHTHOUSE CLOSE.

YOU SUPPORT THE IDEA OF THE MARITIMES MERGING AS LONG AS IT DOESN'T INCLUDE NOVA SCOTIA.

YOU CAN ORDER A TWO PIECE MEAL AT
A&K LICK-A-CHICK WITH A STRAIGHT FACE.

YOU HAVE WAITED FOR NS POWER TO FIX AN OUTAGE ON A NICE CALM DAY.

YOU CAN SEE DOZENS OF UNIQUE SPECIES OF WILDLIFE SIMPLY BY DRIVING TO YARMOUTH.

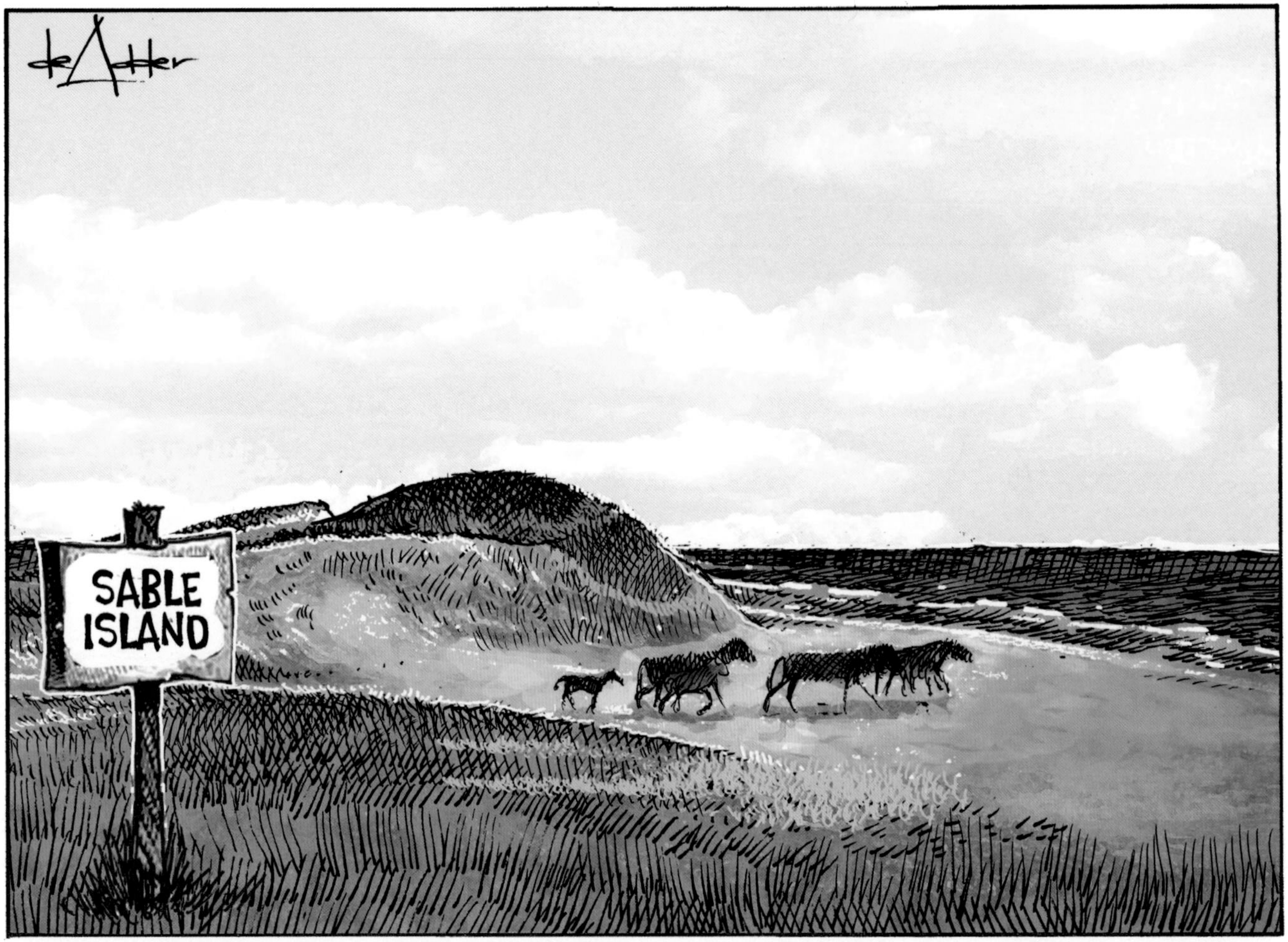
SABLE ISLAND

NO MATTER HOW MANY PLACES IN NOVA SCOTIA YOU'VE SEEN THERE'S ALWAYS ONE PLACE YOU'VE MISSED.

YOU CAN'T WALK ON WATER BUT YOU CAN SNOWMOBILE ON IT.

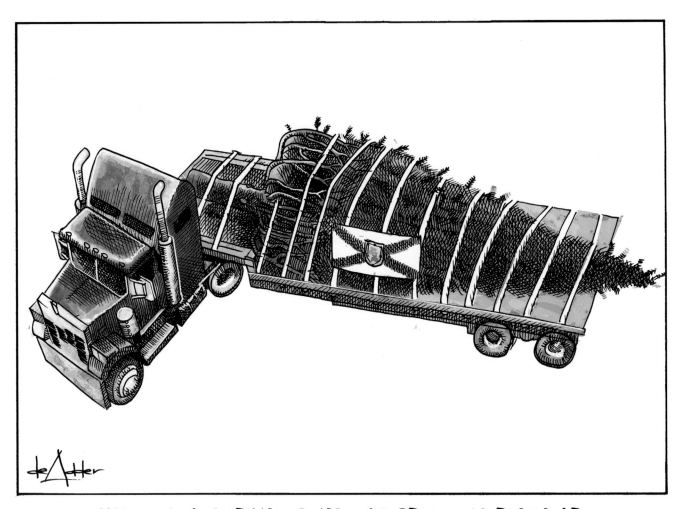

YOU FEEL A STRONG SENSE OF PRIDE EVERY YEAR
WHEN THE CHRISTMAS TREE IS SENT TO BOSTON.

YOU'VE HAD A GOOD TIME AT A FUNERAL.

YOU GO SWIMMING IN JUNE AND YOUR
TESTICLES DECEND IN SEPTEMBER.

THE BIGGEST LOCAL CELEBRITY IN YOUR TOWN
IS THE GUY WHO DRIVES THE ZAMBONI.

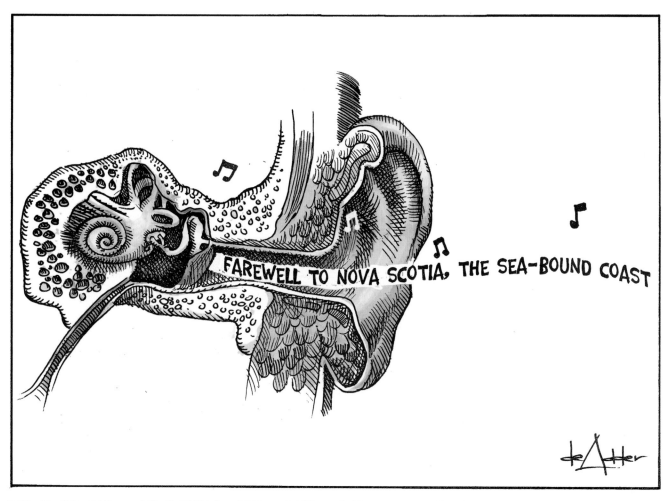

FAREWELL TO NOVA SCOTIA, THE SEA-BOUND COAST

THERE'S ONE EAR WORM YOU DON'T MIND GETTING STUCK IN YOUR HEAD.

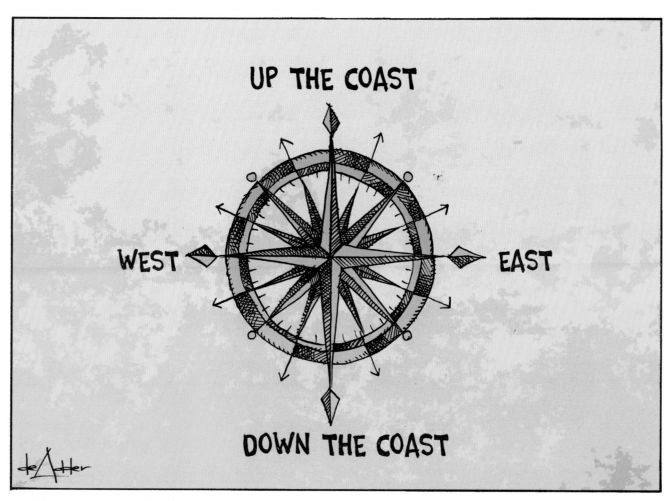

FOR YOU THERE'S NO NORTH OR SOUTH WHEN GIVING DIRECTIONS.

YOU REMEMBER THE PARTY LINE AND SORT OF MISS IT.

YOU PUT THE "KETTLE ON" WHEN COMPANY COMES OVER.

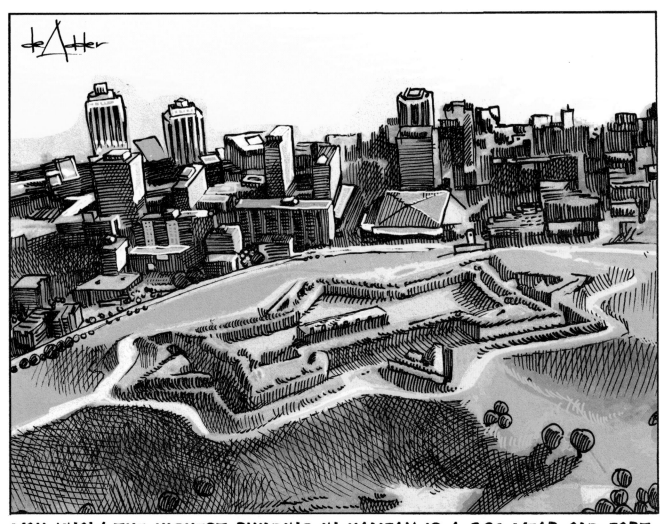

YOU KNOW THE HIGHEST BUILDING IN HALIFAX IS A 260 YEAR OLD FORT.

YOU REMEMBER WHEN SEATTLE WAS THE CENTRE OF THE MUSIC WORLD, AND HALIFAX WAS CONSIDERED THE SEATTLE OF THE NORTH.

YOU HAVE HAD MURDEROUS THOUGHTS
ABOUT SHUBENACADIE SAM.

YOU'VE HAD YOUR PICTURE TAKEN WITH THE COW BAY MOOSE.

IF A GUY ON AN OVERPASS MADE YOUR MORNING.

MISS ALLY

106911

YOU'VE BEEN TOUCHED BY A CREW LOST AT SEA.

YOU GET ASKED "WHAT'S YOUR FATHER'S NAME"
FROM COMPLETE STRANGERS.

WHEN A NEIGHBOUR IS IN TROUBLE,
YOU START BAKING.

YOU FEEL NOVA SCOTIA'S MOTTO SHOULD REFLECT LIFE IN THE PROVINCE.

YOU MAY HAVE GOTTEN A "D" IN MATH, BUT YOU CAN COUNT A CRIB HAND LIKE A HUMAN CALCULATOR.

THE CITY

WHEN YOU SAY YOU'RE GOING TO THE CITY
IT MEANS YOU'RE GOING TO HALIFAX.

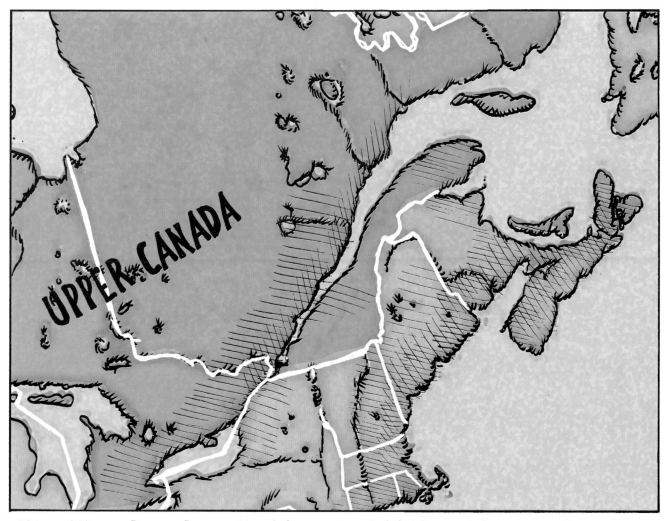

YOU CONSIDER EVERYTHING WEST OF NEW BRUNSWICK UPPER CANADA.

YOU KNOW JUNE IS NOT THE START OF COTTAGE SEASON.

YOU'VE DRIVEN 10 KPH ON THE TRANS-CANADA.

YOU SAW JESUS ON A WALL AT TIM HORTONS.

ON DAYS YOU DON'T HAVE TIME TO READ THE NEWSPAPER,
YOU STILL MAKE TIME TO READ THE OBITUARIES.

YOU KNOW THERE'S ONLY TWO DEGREES OF SEPARATION
BETWEEN YOU AND ANOTHER NOVA SCOTIAN.

YOU KNOW WHAT IT MEANS TO "DRESS A FISH".

YOU REMEMBER PICKING BLUEBERRIES WITH YOUR PARENTS
AND EATING FAR MORE THAN YOU PICKED.

DIGBY SCALLOPS + BACON =

YOU KNOW SOMETHING THAT GOES TOGETHER,
AND IS BETTER THAN PEANUT BUTTER AND JAM.